Contents

Contains over 120 recipes!

Key: Preparation Time in minutes Cooking Time in minutes Combined prep and cooking time

tab - **tablespoon**   tsp - **teaspoon**

Scintillating Starters, Dips and Salsas

Stilton Spread, with Red Pears

Serves 12

125g (4oz) Colston Bassett Stilton

3 tabs whipping cream

30g (1oz) chopped and toasted walnuts

1 ripe (but firm) red pear, thinly sliced.
Bread or crackers of your choice

Lightly blend the Stilton with the whipping cream.

Stir in the walnuts and chill.

Spread over the bread or crackers of your choice and top with the sliced pear.

Ideally served with multi-seeded crackers, crusty bread or hot, toasted bread cut into fingers.

Colston Bassett and District Dairy Ltd.

Garlic Butter

Enough for 1 medium baguette

125g (4oz) unsalted butter, softened

2 peeled cloves of garlic, crushed with a pinch of salt

chopped parsley or tarragon

Cream the butter, mix in the garlic and blend until well combined.

Stir in the herbs. Will keep for a few days in the fridge.

Use as required with breads or with mussels or escargot.

A family recipe

Macadamia Cheese Puffs

Makes about 60 - recipe easily halved

¾ white loaf, unsliced and stale (leave out overnight)

120g (4oz) butter

120g (4oz) each of mature Cheddar and cream cheese

1tsp ready made English mustard – more if you prefer

2 egg whites

120g (4oz) chopped Macadamia nuts

ground black pepper

Pre-heat oven to 200C/400F/Gas 5-6

Remove crusts from bread and cut into 2cm or 1inch cubes.

Put butter, cheeses, mustard and pepper in a basin over a saucepan of gently boiling water (basin should not touch the water) and leave to almost melt. Stir until all ingredients are well combined.

Beat egg whites until stiff and fold into the slightly cooled sauce.

Put the nuts into a shallow container or plate.

Dip the cubes of bread into the sauce mixture, covering all sides.

Then dip the tops of the cubes into the Macadamia nuts.

If using immediately, place on non-stick baking parchment and bake for 10 minutes.

To freeze: do not cook. Place cubes on a tray and open freeze. When frozen pack into airtight containers, with layers of paper separating the cubes.

Quick easy canapés, delicious in summer or winter.

Left over sauce? See next recipe.

Rowena Jones, Queensland, Australia

...a collection of Delicious Sauce Recipes

Macadamia Cheese Puff Toasties

20 **10**

plus grilling time

Makes enough for 4 slices of bread

Left over sauce from the previous recipe

Or: make up half the quantity of sauce from the previous recipe

4 slices of bread, of your choice

Macadamia nuts (optional)

Pre-heat the grill

Spread the sauce thickly over the sliced bread.

Place under the grill until golden and bubbling.

Sprinkle with macadamia nuts (optional) and grill for I minute more. Slice into fingers and serve hot.

Options: put sliced tomatoes over the sauce before grilling.
Quick, easy canapé; tasty supper dish or light lunch served with salad

Rowena and Bunty

Pesto Pizza

10-15 **10-15**

Serves 4 - quick and so easy

2 ready prepared pizza bases from the supermarket

2 large roasted peppers - from a jar is fine

4 to 6 tabs pesto - from a jar is fine

cheese of your choice - grated, sliced or torn

12 olives - optional

Pre-heat oven to 220C/425F/Gas 6-7

Place pizza bases onto oven trays. Thickly spread each with pesto.

Tear the peppers into pieces and arrange on top with the olives.

Scatter some grated or sliced cheese on top.

Bake for 10 -15 minutes until golden and bubbling.

To serve: scatter with rocket leaves and more cheese shavings.
Try using Panini or other types of bread.

Variation of a recipe we enjoyed in a small Italian restaurant.

Leek and Stilton Dip

Serves 4-6 as a supper starter

A little oil and a knob of butter

2 medium size leeks

¼ tsp dried chilli (optional or more if you like it)

½ glass white wine

1 tab chopped tarragon

1 clove of garlic, crushed and finely chopped

200g (7oz) cream cheese

90g (3oz) Stilton cheese, crumbled

30g (1oz) walnuts (or pecans) roughly broken

Pre-heat oven to 180C/360F/Gas 4

Finely slice the leeks. Heat the oil and butter in a pan.

Add the leeks, chilli and a really good glug of wine.

Sauté the leeks until the wine has been absorbed.

Add the garlic and tarragon and cook for 1 minute.

In a bowl, mix the leeks with the cream cheese and Stilton.

Transfer the mixture to a small ovenproof dish (about 6 inches in diameter). Sprinkle the nuts over the top.

Bake for 25-30 minutes until the dip is bubbling.

Serve: spoon into chicory or little gem leaves; celery or warm, toasted ciabatta. Wonderfully rich and creamy.
Try it with grated nutmeg before baking. Try adding crispy bacon on top.

Get ahead and make the day before. Cool, cover with cling film and refrigerate. Sprinkle with the nuts before baking.

Colston Bassett

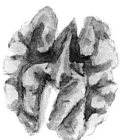

Hot Cheesy Melt

10-15 **30**

Serves 6 – 8

700g (1½lb) bag of frozen chips, of your choice

50g (2oz) Parmesan cheese, grated

25g (1oz) plain flour

1 tsp English mustard powder

300ml (½ pint) milk

140g (5oz) mature Cheddar, grated

½ tsp garlic salt – optional

chopped chives

Pre-heat oven to 220C/400F/Gas 6-7

Spread the chips on a couple of baking trays and cook for 10 -15 minutes. Scatter over half the Parmesan and the garlic salt to coat the chips. Return to the oven and cook for another 10 -15 minutes.

Mix the flour with a little milk. Add the mustard and the rest of the milk and cook gently, whisking until smooth. When sauce is bubbling and thickened, turn off the heat and stir in the rest of the cheese until melted. Season to taste.

Pour into an ovenproof serving bowl and cover with cling film until ready to serve. Gently re-heat in the microwave, stir in the chives and serve as a dipping sauce with the hot chips - and plenty of napkins!

Be aware: there is never enough of this!
Also good with thickly, chipped and roasted sweet potatoes.

From a good, eating pub, in the Vale of Belvoir

Mango Salsa

Serves 4 to 6

½ red onion

½ to 1 whole mango peeled

2 spring onions

12 cherry tomatoes

½ red chilli - more if you wish

good squeeze lime juice;
to your taste

1 to 2 tsps sweet balsamic
vinegar; to your taste

fresh herbs of your choice -
mint, parsley, basil

Finely chop onions, tomatoes, chilli and mango.

Add lime juice to taste and balsamic vinegar.

Add chopped parsley if using.

Stir, chill and leave for flavours to develop.

If using basil and/or mint add just before serving

Fresh and zingy! Good with anything!

Serve on hot, crusty bread, tortillas, fill little gem lettuce leaves or individual chicory leaves....
Also good with cold meats, hot and cold salmon, cold chicken......

Breast Cancer Support Group, Nottingham

...a collection of Delicious Sauce Recipes

Pepper and Tomato Salsa

10-15

Serves 6 to 8

125g (4oz) cherry tomatoes

1 garlic clove, finely chopped

1 red chilli, deseeded and chopped

225g (8oz) roasted red peppers, from a jar is fine

6 to 8 peppadew (from a jar). Add more if you like the heat.

2 tsps sweet balsamic vinegar

1 tab tomato puree (of your choice)

seasoning

Tip all ingredients into a food processor and pulse to a rough puree.

Adjust seasoning and tip into a serving bowl.

Stir and add a glug of olive or rapeseed oil.

Cover with cling film and chill until ready to serve.

Gently stir before serving

Fresh, hot and spicy! Serve with lots of fresh, crusty bread, tortillas or crostini.

Delicious as a dip for large, fresh prawns.

Also good with pasta and also as a marinade for chicken.

Super, sexy salsa!

N.B.C.S.G.

Smoked Mackerel Paté

serves 4

2 large smoked mackerel fillets

200ml (7floz) mayonnaise, homemade or shop bought

3 tabs crème fraîche

1 tsp horseradish sauce

½ lemon, juice only

1 tsp Dijon mustard

freshly ground black pepper

Remove the skin from the mackerel, check for any small bones.

Blend the fish, adding the mayonnaise and crème fraîche gradually.

Add the seasonings, horseradish, mustard, black pepper, and finally the lemon juice, a little at a time so it isn't too sharp

Put into a small serving dish and chill.

Serve with Melba toast or sourdough bread. Good to pack for picnics

Lockett Tomblin, The Plough, Cropwell Butler

Smoked Salmon Dip

Serves 4 generously

80g (3oz) smoked salmon

good squeeze of lime juice

2 tsps capers (rinsed) more if you wish

200g (7oz) cream cheese – medium fat

2 tabs of soured cream or natural yoghurt

chopped dill, tarragon or chives

Place the smoked salmon, lime juice, and capers in a food processor and pulse until roughly chopped.

Add the cream cheese and soured cream and process until all ingredients are combined and the dip is the consistency you prefer.

Serve with fingers of warm brown toast.
Quick, easy and delicious!
Very versatile

Variation of a well known but easy recipe

...a collection of Delicious Sauce Recipes

Salad Cream

Serves 6-8

4 egg yolks

8 level tsps caster sugar

2 tabs plain flour

I tab of English mustard

200ml (6 fl oz) white wine vinegar

300ml (10 fl oz or ½ pint) double cream

Mix all the ingredients in a large bowl, except the double cream.

Cook over a Bain Marie, whisking continuously until the mixture has thickened.

Separately, whip up the double cream until thickened.

Fold the egg mixture into the cream.

Season to taste with salt and lemon juice.

Pot up in sterilised jars and keep in the fridge for up to three days.

A luxurious, homemade, comfort dressing.
Good with poached salmon, trout and anything that takes your fancy!
Dan Burridge, Hart's Restaurant, Nottingham

Tzatziki

Serves 4 to 6

150g (5oz) natural yoghurt

125g (4½ oz) quark
(or light cream cheese)

125g (4½oz) crème fraîche
or sour cream,

dash of lemon juice

2 or 3 cloves garlic (according to taste) crushed

1 small finely chopped onion

¼ cucumber chopped

salt and pepper

Mix all ingredients and leave in the fridge for several hours or overnight. Check seasoning.

Easy and tasty – great with baked potatoes, fresh bread or barbecued meat or fish.
Also low in calories if using low fat yoghurt and half fat crème fraîche.

Sabine Stanley, Tewin

Bramley Apple and Mint Chutney

10 90

plus cooling and potting up

Easy

1.5kg (2½ lbs) Bramley apples, peeled cored and diced

300ml (10 fl oz) malt vinegar

90g (3 oz) light brown sugar

335g (12 oz) granulated sugar

1 tsp salt

50g (1½ oz) sultanas

25g (1 oz) pack fresh mint, chopped

Place all the ingredients except the mint in a large saucepan and bring to the boil. Cover and simmer gently on a medium heat for 1 hour, stirring occasionally.

Remove the lid and stir in the mint. Increase the heat and cook for a further 15 minutes or until thickened

Cool slightly before spooning into sterilised jars, top with a waxed disc and seal with a lid.

Good with cold cuts and cheese

By kind permission of Waitrose 2012

D'ont waste
the Marinade

Dreamy Dressings & Marvellous Marinades

Dill and Mustard Dressing

5

Serves 4
Very quick

1 tab sherry or wine vinegar

2 tsps of sugar

1 tab Dijon mustard

150ml (¼ pint) single cream

large bunch dill, finely chopped

few grinds of black pepper

Simply mix all ingredients together.

Suitable for all fish, especially salmon or trout.
If you like dill, it's also good drizzled over salads or pasta.

Dill....icious!

Colston Bassett Stilton Cheese Dressing

10

Serves 12 - easily halved

225g (8oz) mayonnaise

2 tabs minced onion

1 tab minced garlic (or to your taste)

1 small bunch fresh parsley, chopped

1 tab lemon juice

1 tab white wine vinegar

80g (about 3oz) Colston Bassett Stilton cheese, crumbled

seasoning

Combine all the ingredients in a bowl and mix well.
Cover and refrigerate for at least one hour before serving.

This is a quick, easy and versatile dressing

Colston Bassett and District Dairy

Mango Dressing

Serves 6 - simple

2 ripe Indian mangos (or Thai)

12 basil leaves

4 limes juiced

1 lemon juiced

200ml (8 fl oz) olive oil

pinch salt

Peel and stone the mangos and blitz with the basil leaves and juices of the limes and lemon. Slowly, add the olive oil and blitz.

Pass through a fine sieve and season with salt.

An intensely flavoured dressing which is fantastic with cooked lobsters, crab or prawns. Also has a massive impact on chicken salad.

Dan Burridge, Hart's Restaurant, Nottingham

Oyster Dressing

10-15

Serves 4 - easy but special

5 large native oysters (ask fishmonger to shuck oysters)

2 egg yolks

70 to100ml (3-4 fl oz) olive oil

salt

½ lemon, juice only

Shuck and wash the oysters. Blitz egg yolks and oysters together.
Whilst blitzing add the oil slowly.
Season with lemon juice and salt to taste.

A gourmet dressing. Drizzle around the plate. Great with any cold fish starter or ceviche fish. Goes extremely well with scallops.

Dan Burridge, Hart's Restaurant, Nottingham

5

Honey and Mustard Salad Dressing

Store in the fridge for up to one week.

5 tabs rape seed oil or olive oil

1tsp wholegrain mustard

large drizzle of runny honey (to your taste)

Put all ingredients in a small jug or bowl and whisk with a fork until combined.

Drizzle over salads or use as a dipping sauce with chunks of fresh crusty bread.

Ownsworth's Cold Pressed, Extra Virgin Oil

Mango, Ginger and Garlic Dressing

Store in the fridge for up to one week.

5 tabs rapeseed or olive oil

1 tsp freshly grated ginger

2 cloves of garlic, peeled and crushed - to your taste

1 tab smooth mango chutney

Whisk all ingredients together until combined.

Drizzle over summer salads.
Also good as a marinade for chicken or salmon.

Ownsworth's Cold Pressed Extra Virgin Oils

Roast Lemon Dressing

10-15 **45**

Serves 4 - 6

4 whole lemons

100ml (4fl oz) olive oil

50g (2oz) icing sugar

1 lemon juiced

1 tab English mustard

Pre-heat oven to 120C /250F/Gas1

Wash and dry lemons. Toss in a little olive oil, place on a tray and cover with foil. Bake in oven for 45 minutes until soft.

Chop off the top and scoop out the centre/pulp into a large mixing bowl. Add the icing sugar and mustard and slowly whisk in the olive oil.

Season to taste with lemon juice. Pass through a fine sieve.

One of my favourite dressings. A good all rounder with a zingy, lemon flavour.
Dan Burridge, Hart's Restaurant, Nottingham

John's Elderflower and Lemon Dressing

5

Serves 4 - keeps in the fridge for 1 week

1 tab elderflower cordial

2 tabs olive oil (or oil of your choice)

1 tsp Dijon mustard

good squeeze of lemon juice

seasoning, to taste

Mix all ingredients together in a screw top jar - or jam jar.

Shake until well mixed.

Drizzle over mixed green salad or use as a dip with crusty bread and cheese.
***Excellent with:** crisp salads containing mango, melon or pawpaw.*

***Variations:** add chopped mint or tarragon.*

Add chopped dill and serve with smoked or poached salmon.

John Fletcher

Baked Salmon Marinade

Serves 4
Marinate for 60 minutes

4 salmon fillets

2 tabs grape seed or light oil

3 tabs soft brown sugar

1 lemon, juice only

1 tab fresh ginger, finely chopped

1 clove garlic

freshly ground black pepper

fresh herbs to serve

Pre-heat oven to 180C/360C/Gas 4

Mix all the ingredients together and spoon over the salmon.

Leave to marinate for at least an hour. Strain the marinade from the salmon and put the fish into an ovenproof dish.

Pour the marinade over the salmon and bake for 10-15 minutes.

Serve with new potatoes tossed with the fresh herbs and vegetables of your choice.

This marinade recipe was given to me by my friend Kate Stanton who, unlike me, is a fantastic cook!

Emma Curzon, Kedleston Hall

Spring Onion and Mint Marinade

Serves 4
Marinate for 2 to 3 hours

2 tabs fresh mint, chopped

bunch spring onions, snipped into small pieces

5 tabs balsamic vinegar

5 tabs rape seed oil (or olive oil)

sea salt and ground black pepper

Mix all ingredients for the marinade in a non-metallic bowl.

Place lamb chops or lamb steaks (or chunks of lamb for a barbecue kebab) in the marinade. Cover and leave for 2 to 3 hours in the fridge for the flavours to infuse.

Cook on a barbecue or pre-heated oven for 15 to 20 minutes.

Serve with summer vegetables or couscous. Easy to make and very tasty
Get ahead: *Prepare the ingredients and leave the meat to marinate over night.*

Marinated Tuna Steaks with Herb Butter

Serves 6
Marinate for 1 hour

6 tuna steaks

2 tabs olive oil

2 tabs lemon juice

1 tab sun-dried tomato puree

1 garlic clove, crushed or finely chopped

salt and ground black pepper

Whisk together the olive oil, lemon juice, tomato puree, garlic and seasoning in a large, shallow non-metallic dish.

Place the tuna steaks in the marinade and coat well.

Cover and refrigerate for an hour or so.

Remove the fish from the marinade and grill (or cook on a heated griddle) on a medium to high heat for 4 to 5 minutes on each side, basting with the marinade, until just cooked through.

Do not over-cook.

Wonderful served with a spoonful of herb butter on each steak.
A taste of the Mediterranean

Easy Marinade/ Sauce for Chicken

Serves 4
Marinate for 1 hour or overnight

4 chicken breasts, left whole (if breasts are thick, slice in half lengthways or chunk for BBQ on skewers)

300ml (½ pint) or enough orange juice to cover 4 chicken breasts

150ml (¼ pint) Soy Sauce

good twist black pepper to taste

2 tabs runny honey

1 - 2 crushed cloves garlic (to your taste)

pinch of dried chilli or 1 tab sweet chilli sauce to taste

good glug cooking oil (olive, groundnut, sunflower or similar)

1 tab ready mixed mustard (to help emulsify the mix)

1 tab grated/chopped ginger fresh or from a jar

Whisk up all ingredients, pour over the chicken and leave in fridge for at least 2 hours or overnight.

For cubed chicken: put on skewers and BBQ. Boil remaining marinade to thickening point and use as a sauce.

**For whole chicken breasts:
Pre-heat oven to 180C/360F/Gas 4**

Cook for 20 minutes covered, and further 5 to10 minutes uncovered, to brown chicken a little. Check chicken is cooked.

Serve the marinade as a sauce after boiling for a few minutes.

---

*Delicious with a crisp salad and French bread to soak up the sauce.
Or: mashed/creamed potatoes (rice or noodles) with seasonal veg.*

This is proper "bloke" food. Dead easy to prepare and cook and not too exact on the quantities.

Chris Smith, Gedling

Honey & Mustard Marinade for Steak

15 **VARIES**

Serves 4
Marinate 2 hours or overnight

4 sirloin steaks

4-5 tabs rapeseed or olive oil

2 garlic cloves crushed

3-4 tsps wholegrain mustard

1 tab runny honey

1 tab freshly chopped oregano (or ½ tab dried oregano)

1 tab freshly chopped thyme (or ½ tab dried thyme)

juice of 2 unwaxed lemons

ground black pepper

In a non-metallic bowl, place the steaks along with all the other ingredients. Using a spoon or your hands, thoroughly coat the steaks with the herby oil. Cover the bowl and refrigerate for 2 hours, or overnight, for the flavours to develop.

Cook in a hot frying pan for 2 minutes on each side for rare, 3-4 minutes for medium rare and 6-7 minutes for well done.

If cooking well done, turn the heat down slightly on the hob to ensure that the honey does not burn.

Serve with a summer salad of mixed leaves

Adds a buzz to steak!

Moroccan Paste

10-15

Serves 4 to 6 - easy

120g (4oz) chopped red chillies

3 tsps ground cumin seeds

3 tsps ground coriander seeds

1 tsp ground caraway seeds

3 tabs chopped mint leaves

3 tabs chopped fresh coriander

3 cloves garlic, crushed or minced

2-3 tabs olive oil

juice of half a lemon

½ tsp salt

Put all ingredients into a blender or food processor and whiz to a coarse paste.

Use as a marinade or a sauce to go with meat or chunky vegetables.

Jane Stipinovich, Seychelles

Saucy Sauces

warm and stir
languorously

Mark Huskinson

Amazingly Adaptable Sauces

Ajika (a spicy Russian paste)

10 plus 1 hour to soak the chillies

Makes about 250g of paste

220g of medium hot red chillies

4 fat cloves of garlic

4 tabs of walnuts

½ tsp of rock salt

4 tabs of coriander

Remove the seeds from the chillies and soak in warm water, ideally, for 1 hour, to reduce the heat a little.

Remove the chillies from the water and put all of the ingredients into a food processor. Blitz to a fine paste.

Store in a glass jar and keep refrigerated. Use within three weeks

The above Ajika recipe, is the Abkhazian variant of this popular Russian paste, originating from the Caucasus. Best used sparingly, it is a good accompaniment to cold meats and can be added as a spicy flavouring to stews and casseroles. Mix with crème fraîche for a spicy dip.

Ajika is also used as a rub for roast chicken or a marinade.

The above recipe approximates to 'vindaloo' spiciness but can be toned down to taste, depending on the type and quantity of the chillies.

Svetlana Willmott, Colston Bassett

Barbecue Sauce

15

Serves 4

1 small onion, chopped

3 cloves garlic, crushed

olive oil

1 red chilli, finely chopped

1 tsp fennel seeds, crushed

50g (2oz) dark brown sugar

50ml (1¾fl oz) dark soy sauce

300ml (10fl oz) tomato ketchup

salt and pepper

Soften the onion in olive oil; add the garlic, chilli, fennel seeds and sugar.

Add the soy sauce and ketchup and season with salt and pepper.

Bring to the boil and simmer for a few minutes to combine the flavours.

Use as a dip or to coat spare ribs, chicken or sausages.
Good in the winter with fillet of pork or game

Gilly Cross

Hollandaise Sauce

5 · 20

Serves 6-8

Classic Hollandaise sauce is delicious and has many uses. If you make Hollandaise in advance, keep it in a slightly warm place, but be careful not to put it anywhere too warm, or in the fridge, as it will split.

3 egg yolks

pinch of salt

½ tsp caster sugar

1 tab lemon juice

1 tab white wine

1 tab white wine vinegar

1 shallot, peeled and finely sliced

12 white peppercorns, cracked

175g (6oz) salted butter

Place the egg yolks, salt and sugar in a food processor and give them a quick whiz. In a small pan heat the lemon juice, wine, wine vinegar, shallot and peppercorns together, until the liquid has reduced by half.

Meanwhile, in another pan melt the butter and allow it to bubble but not colour.

Turn on the food processor again and strain in the hot, reduced liquor, followed slowly by the hot butter.

Once all the butter has been added, pour the Hollandaise sauce into a bowl and keep warm, covered with clingfilm, until needed.

Wonderful with eggs Benedict, chicken or fresh asparagus

Celebratory Chef: Galton Blackiston, Morston Hall, North Norfolk.

Herb and Caper Sauce

10

Serves 4

This sauce is so simple it probably doesn't deserve the title of 'recipe'

2 large tabs of capers, rinsed

4 anchovy fillets

1 clove of garlic, roughly chopped

1 tsp English mustard

2 tsps of vinegar (any you like)

1 large handful of parsley or any other herbs

200ml (7fl oz) good quality olive oil

Add all the ingredients except the herbs and olive oil into a food processor. Blend until smooth.

Add the herbs and pulse to chop but not completely puree, while adding the olive oil.

It can be taken to a smooth sauce or left coarse.

If you don't wish to use a food processor it can be done in a mortar and pestle, but the herbs need to be chopped finely with a kitchen knife.

This will sit quite happily in the fridge for up to a week, but the vivid green colour will start to fade after 46 hours or so.
Serve over pasta; firm fleshed fish or cold meats. Very adaptable.

The Larder at Goosegate, Nottingham.

Basic White Sauce (Béchamel)

15-20

Makes about 600ml or 1 pint

60 g (2-3 oz) butter

45g (1½ oz) plain flour

600ml (1pint) milk

seasoning

Gently heat the butter over a low heat. Remove from the heat.

Add the flour whisk to make a smooth paste (or roux).

Add about 150 ml (¼ pint) milk and beat well with the whisk.

Once smooth add the remaining milk.

Return the pan to the heat and bring the white sauce gently to a boil, whisking continuously. Once the sauce bubbles and thickens, reduce the heat to allow the flour to "cook out".

Add seasoning.

Strain if necessary before serving.

A classic sauce with variations...

Cheese Sauce

Add 115-225g (4-6oz) of grated cheese and 1 tsp mustard once sauce is cooked. Cheeses that melt easily or Stilton are ideal.

Cream Sauce

Replace some of the milk with single cream. Add grated nutmeg.

Mustard Sauce

Stir in 1 tab of Dijon or whole grain mustard with a pinch of sugar.

Mushroom Sauce

Sauté 225g (8oz) sliced chestnut mushrooms in a little oil or butter until softened, then add to the sauce.

Parsley Sauce

Add 2 tabs fresh parsley (more if you wish) and a few gratings of nutmeg.

Onion Sauce

Serves 2-4

30g (1oz) butter

240g (8 oz) chopped onions

15g (½oz) plain flour

63ml (2½fl oz) milk

63ml (2½fl oz) single cream

salt and white pepper

grated nutmeg

Heat the butter and add the onion, cover and simmer over a low heat for about 10 minutes. When the onion is tender and transparent mix in the flour and cook for a few minutes.

Add the milk and cream gradually and bring to the boil. Season with salt and pepper and grate over the nutmeg (about 6 gratings - to taste)

Pass through a sieve or blend in a liquidiser. Serve in a sauceboat.

For a chunky sauce omit the sieving.
Serve as an accompaniment for roast lamb and beef with mushrooms.... but not with added gravy!

Great nutmeggy taste!

Ray Wood.

Sauce Soubise (onion sauce)

Makes about 1 pint of sauce

450g (1lb) sliced onions

90g (3oz) butter

40g (1½ g) plain flour

150ml (5fl oz) double cream

400ml (12fl oz) milk or white stock

salt and white pepper

fresh nutmeg

Melt the butter in heavy based saucepan and add the sliced onions.

Cook slowly with the lid on for about 20 minutes, until the onions are tender but not browned. Can press a sheet of wet greaseproof paper on the top of the onions to stop them burning.

Add the flour to the onions and stir over a low heat for 3 minutes to cook the flour through.

Add the milk or stock off the heat, blending well. Put back on the heat and simmer for 15 minutes, stirring occasionally. Sieve or puree in a blender, cool a little, and then add the cream and the seasonings.

Good with eggs, chicken, lamb or vegetables
Jill Wagstaff, Barn Cottage, Diseworth

Minted Pea and Watercress Sauce

Serves 6

425ml (15fl oz) vegetable stock

200g (7oz) potatoes

90g (3oz) watercress

1tab fresh mint

200g (7ozs) frozen peas

salt and pepper

Bring the vegetable stock up to a boil in a medium sized pan.

Chop the potatoes into small cubes and add to the boiling stock, simmer for 30 minutes.

Chop up the watercress and mint.

Add to the stock pan with frozen peas, simmer for a few seconds (cooking too long will lose the green colour). Remove from the heat.

Blend the sauce. Taste for seasoning, adding salt and pepper if necessary. The potatoes in the stock will thicken the sauce.

Coat over salmon, trout, chicken or pasta for a delicious fresh sauce.

A country gardener

...a collection of Delicious Sauce Recipes

Parmesan Cheese Sauce

Serves 6 people.

1 garlic clove, peeled and crushed with a knife, but kept whole

400ml (15fl oz) crème fraîche

200g (7oz) Parmesan cheese grated

2 large free-range organic eggs

sea salt and freshly ground black pepper

Have ready on the hob, a pan half filled with simmering water.

Using a metal or glass bowl, rub round the inside with the whole crushed clove of garlic. Pour in the crème fraîche, the Parmesan cheese and the egg yolks. Place the bowl over the pan of water. Be careful: don't let the bowl touch the water. Whisk gently all the time. Turn off the heat under the pan if the water underneath becomes too hot. **Do not rush this.**

A low heat is essential or the sauce will split.

When thickened, season with salt and pepper.

A lovely vegetarian pasta supper. Good served with tagliatelle, cooked with thickly sliced asparagus and extra grated Parmesan cheese. Good coated over vegetables. From Italy

Warm Tomato Sauce

Serves 2 - easily doubled

150ml (5fl oz or ¼ pint) olive oil

1 small red onion finely chopped

1 lemon, juice only

2 large ripe tomatoes, skinned, and roughly chopped

chopped basil and chervil

seasoning

Gently warm the olive oil. Add onion and cook until soft.

Add tomatoes and lemon and cook through.

Add basil, herbs and seasoning.

Serve immediately.

Lovely with grilled or baked fish, chicken or lamb. Good with pasta or warm roasted vegetables.

Imogen Skirving, Langar Hall, Nottinghamshire

Tomato Ketchup

plus 1 hour baking

1kg (2 lbs) vine ripened tomatoes

150g (5oz) soft brown sugar

1 tsp ground white pepper

3 level tsps Maldon sea salt

splash olive oil

6 garlic cloves, crushed

1 small bunch basil

1 litre (1¾ pints) tomato juice

Pre-heat oven to 200C/400F/Gas 6

Roughly chop tomatoes and toss together with the olive oil, brown sugar, pepper and salt. Spread tomatoes on to a baking tray and bake for 1 hour, stirring at least once or twice, until soft and caramelised.

Transfer into a large pan. Add garlic, basil and tomato juice.

Cook on a fairly high heat and reduce until thick.

Blitz in a food processor until chunky and season to taste.

A chunky, home made ketchup, maximising flavour and simple to make.
Keeps in the fridge for a week.
Dan Burridge, Hart's Restaurant, Nottingham

Brian's Spicy Brown Sauce

1.5 kg (3lbs) red tomatoes

200g (7oz) onions

250g (9oz) brown sugar

250g (9oz) raisins

350g (12oz) chopped dates

25g (1oz) ground ginger

5-10g (½oz chilli powder (adjust to taste)

1 litre (1¾ pints) vinegar

season to taste

Chop tomatoes into small pieces.

Add all the ingredients into a large pan.

Simmer until soft and the sugar has melted.

Blitz in a food processor or pass through a sieve.

Return the sauce to the pan and reduce until it is brown sauce consistency.

Bottle and seal immediately.
Brian

...a collection of Delicious Sauce Recipes

Sauce Choron

5 **20**

Serves 6

225g (8oz) butter

1 tab white wine

2 tabs white wine vinegar

2 egg yolks

salt and cayenne pepper to taste

lemon juice to taste

2 tabs tomato ketchup

To clarify the butter, melt it in a small pan, and then carefully tip out

the golden oil, leaving the milky residue, which you can discard.

Put the wine and wine vinegar into a non-reactive pan.

Bring to the boil, then turn the heat down and reduce until only a tablespoon is left in the pan.

Take off the heat.

Stir in the egg yolks. Then slowly pour in the clarified butter, whisking all the time, until all the butter is absorbed and the sauce starts to thicken.

Season with salt and a little cayenne to taste. Add some lemon juice also to taste. Then add 1 tab of the ketchup and if you want a stronger flavour add the second spoonful.

Delicious served with eggs, pasta, fish or chicken.

Mikael Paylor, The Stafford Hotel, London, by Kempinski

Wild Mushroom Sauce

15 **30-35**

Serves 4

2 tabs oil

8 shallots, finely chopped

175g (6oz) wild mushrooms or chestnut mushrooms

1 crushed clove garlic

few sprigs of thyme

1 tab Cognac

300ml (½ pint) Madeira wine

220ml (8fl oz) chicken or vegetable stock

2 tabs double cream

1 knob butter

squeeze lemon juice to taste

Gently, heat oil in a pan. Add shallots and mushrooms.

Leave until caramelised, stirring occasionally.

Add thyme and garlic.

Deglaze pan with cognac (make sure that all brandy is burnt off)

Add Madeira. Add stock and simmer for 20 minutes.

Raise heat and whisk in cream and a knob of butter.

Season and add lemon juice to taste.

Excellent with chicken, game or fowl.

Also as a vegetarian option with rice or pasta

The Martins Arms, Colston Bassett

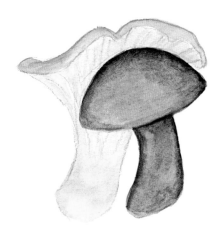

Perfect Pasta

Fettuccini with Ricotta Dressing and Summer Vegetables

15 | **10-15 for Pasta**

Serves 4 - speedy, pasta supper

250g (9oz) fettuccine

200g (7oz) young French beans

4 courgettes, thinly sliced

200g (7oz) Ricotta

4 tabs olive oil

4 tabs lemon juice

salt and black pepper

cherry tomatoes

1 yellow pepper, thinly sliced

Cook the pasta according to the packet instructions.

Blanch the beans and courgettes for 2-3 minutes and refresh in cold water.

Make the dressing: mix the ricotta with the olive oil, lemon juice, salt and pepper.

Reserve a cup of the cooking water and drain the fettuccine.

Add the beans and courgettes. Toss with the dressing until well coated, adding a little of the pasta water if necessary.

Divide between 4 warm bowls and top each serving with a few cherry tomatoes, fresh basil leaves, the sliced pepper and shavings of Parmesan...and a twist of black pepper.

Pour a glass of wine and enjoy!

As a variation: sprinkle with grilled crispy bacon or fried sliced mushrooms. Use seasonal vegetables of your choice – such as asparagus.

Recipe from New Zealand

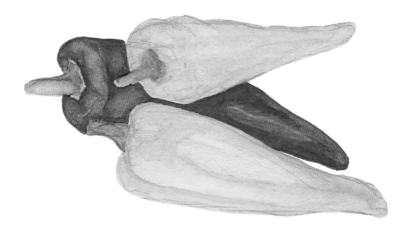

Noodles with Mushrooms and Boursin cheese

20 20

Serves 4 - 5, can easily double up for a party

125g (4 oz) noodles

1½ tabs olive oil

1 small onion, chopped

1 rasher of bacon, chopped

75g (3 oz) mushrooms sliced

1 clove garlic, crushed

1 rounded tab fresh chopped parsley

60g (2½ oz) cream cheese with garlic and herbs

1 tab dry white breadcrumbs

1 tab freshly grated Parmesan cheese

15g (½ oz) butter

salt and freshly milled black pepper

Cook the noodles according to the packet instructions

Meanwhile pre-heat the grill. Heat the oil in another large pan and fry the onion and bacon in the hot oil for 4-5 minutes until lightly coloured. Stir in the mushrooms and cook for another 3-4 minutes, add the crushed garlic. Turn the heat off under the pan, sprinkle with the chopped parsley and season with salt and pepper.

Quickly drain the noodles and transfer them to the large pan containing the onions and mushrooms. Add in the cream cheese, put the lid on the pan and leave for a few minutes to allow the cheese to melt into the mixture.

Taste for seasoning, and then transfer the noodles to a lightly buttered baking dish. Mix the breadcrumbs with the Parmesan cheese and sprinkle over the top of the noodles, dot the surface with flecks of butter and brown under the grill.

Serve with a fresh green salad and garlic bread. Wonderful!
Vegetarian option: leave out the bacon

A holiday recipe

Provençale Sauce

15 **20-25**

Serves 2 generously

450g (1lb) peeled tomatoes, fresh or tinned

1 Spanish onion

1 glass of dry white wine

60ml (2fl oz) olive oil

2 cloves of garlic crushed

sprig of fresh thyme

sprig of fresh rosemary

salt

freshly ground black pepper

Peel and slice the onion. Roughly chop the tomatoes.

Crush the garlic with a little salt.

Sauté the onions in the oil until transparent. Add the garlic.

Toss in the herbs followed by the wine and bring briefly to the boil.

Finally add the tomatoes and seasoning.

Simmer for 15 minutes or until well reduced.

Very good with courgettes or pasta dishes.
Classic: from the South of France

Homemade Pesto Sauce

10

Serves 4

50g (2oz) fresh basil leaves

1 large clove of garlic, crushed

1 tab pine nuts

6 tabs extra virgin olive oil

25g (1oz) Pecorino Romano cheese, grated

pinch of salt

In a blender put the basil, garlic, pine nuts and olive oil together with a pinch of salt. Blend until you have a smooth puree. Transfer the puree to a bowl and stir in the cheese.

A quick sauce for pasta when short of time.
Needs extra cheese to sprinkle on top.

Gorgeous!

Katie Kemp

Pasta Carbonara

Serves 3-4

250g (9oz) pasta of your choice

125ml (4fl oz) double cream

3 egg yolks

50g (2oz) Parmesan cheese, freshly grated

2 tabs (more if you wish) freshly chopped herbs, tarragon,

parsley or chives

salt and pepper

Cook the pasta according to the packet instructions.

Mix the cream, eggs, herbs and seasoning.

Drain the pasta (but leave fairly wet).

Put the egg mixture in the same pan and then return the drained pasta. Stir thoroughly but gently over a moderate heat.

The egg should begin to cook and thicken slightly but do not let the egg become scrambled. Gently, mix in the Parmesan and herbs.

Serve in warm bowls with an extra sprinkling of Parmesan, a twist or two of pepper, chopped herbs, a tomato and rocket side salad ....
.....and a bottle of robust wine! Sooo...satisfying!

An Italian restaurant in Florida

Quickest Cheese Sauce

A few mins

Serves 4 - easily doubled

1 tub crème fraîche

grated cheese; mature Cheddar is best

mustard of your choice

seasoning

Slowly warm the crème fraîche.

Add the grated cheese (to your taste) salt and pepper, a little mustard and stir, gently, until melted. Serve!

Perfect for a quick supper coated over pasta or vegetables

Catherine White of Catherine's Dress Shop, Southwell

...a collection of Delicious Sauce Recipes

Rocket Pesto

10

Serves 4 - Very easy

75g (3oz) wild rocket leaves

125g (4oz) walnuts

8 tabs rapeseed oil

50g (2oz) Parmesan, finely grated

Whizz all ingredients in a food processor until combined and almost smooth.

Ideal for pasta or fresh, green spring vegetables.
Also good drizzled over roasted lamb, chicken, salmon or cod.
A traditional, Italian, peppery sauce

Green Sauce Spaghetti

5-10 **12-15**

Serves 4

400g (14oz) spaghetti

100g bag baby spinach

140g (5oz) frozen peas

small bunch basil, leaves only (reserve a few)

3 tabs green pesto - from a jar is fine

150ml (5fl oz or ¼ pint) single cream

50g (2oz) Parmesan cheese, freshly grated

a little extra cheese for serving

Cook the spaghetti according to the packet instructions.

Boil a kettle. Put the spinach and peas into a bowl and cover with boiling water. Leave for 3-4 minutes, until peas are tender.

Drain well. Tip into a blender or food processor; add the basil, cream and cheese. Blitz to a smooth paste.

Reserve a little of the pasta water, then drain the pasta and return to the pan, over a low heat. Pour the sauce over the pasta and heat through for a few minutes, until the pasta is coated.

Add a little pasta water if it looks too dry.

Serve in warm bowls with extra Parmesan, basil leaves and a few twists of black pepper. Easy and utterly satisfying!

Traditional, Italian recipe

Romesco Sauce

Serves 4 to 6 - very easy, very adaptable

2-3 fresh Romesco peppers, halved and seeds removed

1 red chilli - seeds removed (optional)

2-3 red peppers, quartered and seeds removed

6 large ripe tomatoes, quartered

1-2 red onions

4 cloves garlic unpeeled

50g (2oz) toasted almonds (or ground almonds)

¾ tab wine vinegar or balsamic vinegar

300ml (10fl oz, ½ pint) olive oil – approx measurement

seasoning

Pre-heat oven to 220C/425F/Gas 6-7

Place peppers, garlic and tomatoes in a large oven proof dish or tray. Coat vegetables with some of the oil and bake until gently charred. Leave to cool. Squeeze the garlic from the skins. Put all vegetables into a food processor or blender.

Blend well until smooth.

Add the almonds.

With the motor still running, gradually add the oil and vinegar and continue to blend until the sauce is smooth and well mixed.

Taste and adjust seasoning.

Store in the fridge for up to three days.

Very easy – thick and creamy, bright and beautiful. Works well as a relish; with pasta, baked aubergines, roasted vegetables, between lasagna layers or anything of your choice.

From an Italian/American friend

Basil Cream Sauce

20-25

Serves 2 - easily doubled

175ml (6fl oz) double cream

150g (5oz) butter cut into cubes

squeeze of lemon juice

2 tabs chopped basil

seasoning

Bring cream almost to boiling point, then reduce the heat and simmer until reduced to about 4 tabs and very thick.

Remove from the heat, cool for 1 minute, whisk in the butter bit by bit.

Season with salt, pepper and lemon juice, and stir in the basil

This is a very rich, thick sauce; can be thinned down with a little of the cooked pasta water. Good with any type of pasta.
Add chopped spring onions, peas or asparagus for added crunch.

Jenny Galloway

Walnut Sauce for Pasta

10   (10-15

Serves 2 – quick and easy to prepare

75g (2½oz) walnut halves

3 garlic cloves

handful fresh chives and parsley

2 tabs crème fraîche

2 tabs grated Parmesan cheese

enough pasta for 2 people

handful of rocket leaves

Cook the pasta according to the packet instructions.

Whizz half the walnut halves with the garlic clove in a food processor.

Add the fresh herbs, stir in the crème fraîche and 1 tab of the Parmesan cheese.

Drain the pasta and stir into the sauce together with the remaining walnuts, chopped and sprinkled on top, and the last tablespoon of Parmesan cheese.

An unusual pasta sauce, with added crunch.
Serve garnished with chopped chives or spring onions.
Italian recipe

Pasta with Fillet Steak, Brandy and Cream

10 **10-15**

Serves 4 - speedy pan fry for pasta

4 fillet steaks

oil and butter for pan frying

4 tabs brandy

4 tabs double cream

salt and black pepper

Cook the pasta, of your choice, according to the manufacturer's instructions.

Heat 2 tabs oil in a heavy frying pan and add the butter.

Add the steak and cook for 3 minutes on each side (longer if you prefer). Remove to a serving plate and keep warm.

Deglaze the pan with the brandy. Add the cream.

Boil the sauce while stirring and season to taste.

Drain the pasta and serve into warm bowls. Place the steak on top and pour the sauce over the steak and pasta.

Garnish with chopped chives or basil.

Or before cooking: you might prefer to cut the steak into slices (thick or thin) and stir fry quickly.
To serve, toss the pasta into the steak and sauce until each strand is well coated.

Vegetarian option: use mushrooms, roasted peppers or tomatoes, pine nuts... endless choices!

Recipe from New Zealand

...a collection of Delicious Sauce Recipes

Delicious Pasta Sauce

15 **20**

Serves 4

240g (8ozs) streaky bacon, rind removed and diced

240g (8ozs) mushrooms of your choice, chopped

50g (2ozs) butter

40g (1½ozs) flour

300ml (½pt) milk

150ml (¼pt) double cream

salt and pepper

175ml (6ozs) pasta of your choice

grated Parmesan cheese to serve

Cook the pasta according to the packet instructions.

Dry fry the bacon in a frying pan until crispy, melt a good knob of the butter in a saucepan, cook the mushrooms.

Melt the rest of the butter in the saucepan; add the bacon to the mushrooms. Take off the heat, add the flour and gradually stir in the milk. Put back on to the heat and stir until it thickens. Boil for 2-3 minutes, while still stirring, to reduce and cook out the flour.

Season to taste with salt and pepper. Stir in the cream and reduce until a good consistency i.e. the sauce will coat the back of a spoon.

To serve: mix with the cooked pasta; hand round the Parmesan cheese separately.

This sauce is excellent for vegetarians with the bacon omitted, and the addition of precooked leeks, peppers or by adding asparagus in at the end, when in season.

Also very good with prawns added at the last minute.

D. Bond, Burgage Manor, Southwell

Notes

Fabulous Fish

Prawns on Pawpaw and Avocado

20-25

Serves 6 - each recipe may be served separately

Chives, lime and yoghurt dressing

150ml (5fl oz or ¼ pint) natural yoghurt

1 lime, juice and grated zest

1 tsp mustard - your choice

1 tab chives, chopped

1 tab white wine vinegar

1 tsp sugar

salt and freshly ground black pepper

Mix all the ingredients together about 2 hours in advance and put in the fridge until needed.

For the salsa

300g (18) large ready cooked prawns (de-veined)

1 red chilli, finely chopped

30g (1oz) fresh coriander or parsley leaves

1 tab olive oil

1 pawpaw, cut into balls or cubes

2 ripe avocados, sliced

1 lime, juice and finely grated zest

cucumber ribbons

Mix the prawns, chopped chilli, coriander, olive oil and season to taste. Mix the pawpaw and avocado with the lime juice and zest, then divide among the glasses.

Twist the cucumber ribbons on top for an attractive garnish.

Drizzle the dressing over each serving and serve with extra lime wedges.

Serve as a starter or light lunch. The stuff of dreams when served with a fresh, dry sparkling wine, or a fruity Sauvignon Blanc.
Vegetarian option? Leave out the prawns – it's just as good!
If pawpaw is unavailable, mango is a good substitute.

Recipe from South Africa

Horseradish and Mustard Cream

Serves 4 – easily doubled

1 to 2 tabs horseradish sauce (depends whether it's extra hot)

2 to 3 tabs lemon juice or dry Vermouth

3 tabs crème fraîche or mayonnaise

2 tsps grain mustard

twist of black pepper

Mix everything together and chill until ready to use. Simple!

Good with smoked mackerel, broken into chunks, tiny, hot new potatoes mixed with the cream and served on a bed of salad leaves.

Christine P. Smith, Gedling

Creole Sauce

Serves 4

2 onions diced

2 green peppers diced

1 tsp grated ginger

1 tsp minced garlic

4 ripe tomatoes, chopped

1 tab tomato puree

300ml (½ pint) water or veg stock

juice of half lemon

few sprigs of thyme

salt and pepper to taste

Fry onion and pepper in a little oil until onion is translucent.
Add garlic and ginger and fry briefly.
Add tomatoes and cook for 2 minutes.
Add tomato puree and cook for 5 minutes
Add water or stock. Bring to the boil and cook until thickened.
Add lemon juice and thyme as you serve.

A traditional recipe served with fish.

From Cliff Pool in the Seychelles

Brown Shrimp Béarnaise

Serves 6-8

1 quantity Hollandaise sauce ('Adaptable Sauces' page 31)

125 g (4oz) brown shrimps, peeled

2 tabs chopped fresh tarragon

Make the Hollandaise sauce, then, just before serving, stir in the shrimps and tarragon.

Brown shrimp Béarnaise goes particularly well with skate wings and most wet fish.

Galton Blackiston

Fish Veloute (sauce)

Serves 4

50g (2oz) button mushrooms finely sliced

2 shallots, finely chopped

25g (1oz) unsalted butter

115ml (4fl oz) dry white wine

300ml (10fl oz) fish stock

300ml (10fl oz) double cream

lemon juice to taste

Melt the butter in the pan. Fry the mushrooms and shallots gently to soften. Add the wine and boil until nearly evaporated. Add the stock and boil until reduced by half. Add cream and reduce until the sauce will coat the back of a spoon. Season to taste. Coat over fish and serve

A good supper party dish.

Serve with firm white fish and seasonal vegetables.
Jenny Kaye

Passion and Combava Ocean Sauce

12-15

Serves 4

juice of 4 passion fruits

½ Combava lemon, juice only*

½ onion chopped

6 peppercorns crushed

55ml (2fl oz) of clean seawater*

200g (7oz) butter cut in big cubes*

salt, to taste

Place peppercorns, onion, lemon juice and passion fruit juice in a small saucepan. Put on a lowish heat and reduce by two thirds.

Remove from the heat and strain. Wash the saucepan and return the reduced liquid to the pan.

Add the seawater and bring the mixture to the boil. Remove from the heat and slowly incorporate the butter cube by cube.

The sauce should be shiny and not runny. Check seasoning.

For that final island touch, add grated Combava zest to your taste.

Chef's tip:

"*This fantastic island gourmet sauce marries well with grilled white flesh fish or pan fried seafood*"

*Or use a ripe lemon from the supermarket
*Fresh water and sea salt (Maldon is good) may be substituted.
*Use less butter if you prefer.

Chef: Marcus Freminot, Seychelles

White Wine Cream Sauce

Serves 6

2 shallots chopped finely

20g (¾oz) butter

20g (¾oz) plain flour

200ml (7fl oz) whipping cream

250ml (8fl oz) white wine

salt and pepper

Melt the butter in a saucepan over a gentle heat and cook the shallots until soft and golden - about 5 minutes. Add the flour and stir in while cooking for 1-2 minutes.

Take the saucepan off the heat and gradually add the wine and cream.

Return to the heat and bring to the boil. Whisk thoroughly, until you have a thin, creamy sauce. Season to taste.

Particularly good served over fish

Hilary Kenworthy, Colston Bassett

Dill Sauce

Serves 6 - 8

1 cucumber

4 tsps salt

300ml (10fl oz) mayonnaise

300ml (10fl oz) whipping cream

½ lemon

salt and freshly ground black pepper

4 tabs snipped dill

Peel and dice cucumber, put on a small plate, sprinkle with salt and stand for 30 minutes. Rinse thoroughly.

Blend mayonnaise and cream gently. Stir in lemon juice and seasoning, cucumber and dill.

Serve chilled.

Very good with cold salmon or smoked salmon. Good also with prawns. Can easily double up the quantities. Also good served as a dip.

Traditional recipe – dill...icious!

Coconut Sauce for Trout

15 **20**

Serves 4

50g (2oz) butter

½ onion, finely chopped

2cm (¾ inch) fresh root ginger, peeled and grated

½ lime, zest only

2 tsps plain flour

125ml (4fl oz) white wine

200ml (7fl) oz coconut milk

4-5 tabs fresh basil leaves

Heat the butter in a frying pan over a medium heat. Add the onion, and soften for 2 minutes, add the ginger and lime zest and fry for another minute, then sprinkle in the flour. Add the wine and boil for 2-3 minutes, until the liquid has reduced by half.

Pour in the coconut milk and simmer for 5 minutes. Stir in the basil leaves at the last minute and serve.

Coat over trout fillets, salmon or any white fish

Serve with asparagus, in season, or seasonal vegetables.

Vegetarian option: instead of fish, serve with asparagus and/or spring vegetables.

Gilly Cross

Salmon in Coriander and Lime

Serves 4

4 salmon fillets

zest and juice of 1 lime

2 tsps clear blended honey

2 tsps root ginger, grated

3 tabs olive oil

2 tabs coriander

Pre-heat oven to 200°C/400°F/Gas 6

Place the salmon fillets in a small roasting tin.

Mix together the lime zest and juice, honey, grated ginger, olive oil and finely chopped coriander.

Pour over the salmon, leave to marinate for 10 minutes.

Cover the salmon with foil, and cook for 15 minutes, until fish looks opaque and flakes easily.

Serve with new potatoes & seasonal vegetables.
Also good with tuna steaks

An anonymous friend!

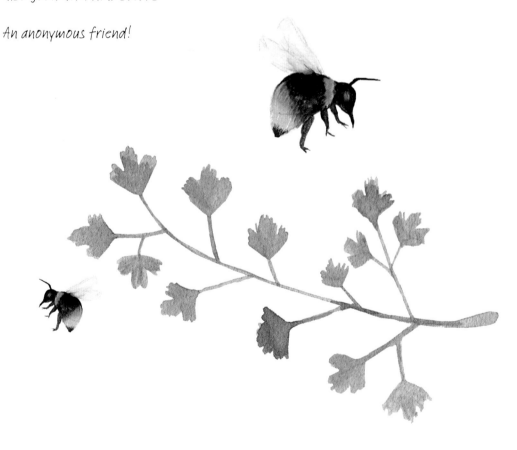

Elderflower and White Wine Fish Sauce

30 **20**

Serves 4
For poaching

4 trout fillets, trimmed and de-boned

150ml (5fl oz) dry white wine

150ml (5fl oz) water

150ml (5fl oz) elderflower pressé

3 slices lemon

3 large sprigs parsley

½ onion, sliced

½ tsp salt

1 tsp whole peppercorns

1 bay leaf

Place the fillets of trout in a shallow lidded pan so liquid is covering the fish and add all the other ingredients. Bring to the boil.

Remove from the heat and allow to cool.

Skin the trout before serving.

Make a Béchamel sauce
(Adaptable Sauces, page 33)

For the parsley sauce: pour 150ml (¼ pint) of the poaching liquid (more if you wish) out of the pan, ready to make a parsley sauce.

1-2 heaped tabs chopped parsley leaves. Chop stalks separately

½ tsp lemon juice

nutmeg for grating

Place the parsley stalks in a bowl. Add hot elderflower pressé and white wine poaching stock. Leave to stand for 5 minutes.

Strain and reserve liquid. Pour into the hot Béchamel sauce and stir well. Add remaining parsley and a few gratings of nutmeg.

Serve the trout with the sauce and seasonal vegetables. This delicious sauce begins with the poaching liquid. It was created when cooking brown trout but also works well with other fish.

Mark Carr, Woodpecker's Catering

Vermouth Sauce

Serves 4

40g (1½oz) shallots

1 sprig of thyme

½ bay leaf

115ml (4fl oz) Noilly Prat or dry Vermouth

300ml (10fl oz) fish stock (or veg. stock)

2 tabs double cream

pinch of paprika

50g (2oz) unsalted butter, chilled

salt and pepper

Simmer shallots, thyme, bay leaf and Vermouth, until reduced by half.

Pour in fish stock, and cook over a medium heat for 10 minutes.

Add the cream, and reduce until it coats the back of a spoon.

Remove thyme and bay leaf.

Turn the heat to low, whisk in the paprika, making sure the sauce doesn't boil. Whisk in the butter. Coat over the fish.

Serve with white fish or shellfish; good with lightly sautéed scallops.

Jenny Kaye

Notes

Fair Game, Chicken, Duck...

Apple and Chestnut Sauce

20-30 40

Serves 4

4 pheasant breasts
- partridge or chicken

packet of sliced pancetta

4 dessert apples, peeled and sliced

15-20 chestnuts
- ready prepared is fine

300ml (½ pint) cider

300ml (½ pint) chicken stock

1 tab icing sugar

double cream

vegetable oil for cooking

seasoning

Season breasts with salt and pepper and wrap in pancetta.

Brown in a pan, with the oil, for about 20 minutes. Brown evenly, don't let them burn. Remove from the pan and keep warm.

Add the sliced apples to the pan and allow them to gently colour.

Add the icing sugar and caramelise.

Remove from pan. Add chestnuts and cook for 2 minutes.

Add the cider and reduce until approximately a third of the liquid remains. Then, add the chicken stock and a good glug of cream. Stir and return the pheasant breasts and apple slices to the sauce. Cook, gently for a further 10-15 minutes.

Serve with creamed, mashed potatoes and seasonal vegetables.

Wonderful, winter comfort food!

Nigel Smith – Gamekeeper
Buckminster Estate

Cheat's Chicken Carbonara

Serves 6

2 x 340g jars of Carbonara pasta sauce

6 medium sized skinned chicken breasts

3 chopped leeks

170 - 225g (6 - 8oz) diced, lean smoked bacon

Pre-heat oven to 160°C/320F/Gas 3

Place the chicken breasts in a casserole dish, put on the lid and cook in the oven for 35 minutes.

In the meantime, fry the bacon until lightly browned. Add the leeks and cook until still soft but holding their shape. Put to one side.

Remove the chicken from the oven, drain off the stock and add the two jars of carbonara sauce, the leeks and the bacon. Season lightly with black pepper, stir and return to the oven for another 35 minutes.

Really easy and delicious.

Works well in a slow cooker.

Elaine Burgin

Crunchy Satay Sauce

5-10   15

Serves 4

1 tab vegetable oil

1 clove garlic peeled, crushed and finely chopped

2 tsps chilli powder (to your taste)

225g (8oz) crunchy peanut butter

1 tab dark Muscavado sugar

zest of a large lemon

300ml (½ pint) warm water

Heat the oil in a saucepan and add the garlic and chilli powder. Cook, stirring for 2 minutes.

Add peanut butter, sugar and lemon zest with the water.

Bring to the boil and simmer for 4 to 5 minutes or until the sauce thickens.

Good with barbecued chicken.
***Vegetarian option:** use Quorn instead of chicken.*

Researched and updated by Joan Bryan

Tarragon Sauce

10   30

Serves 2 - easily doubled

2 shallots, peeled and finely chopped

50g (2oz) unsalted butter

2 tabs white wine vinegar

100ml (3fl oz) dry white wine

300ml (10fl oz) chicken stock

100ml (3fl oz) double cream

salt and pepper, preferably white pepper

5 tabs chopped tarragon leaves

Sweat the shallots in half the butter till softened.

Deglaze the pan with the white wine vinegar and wine, and reduce by half. Pour in the stock and, again, reduce until syrupy.

Add the cream and boil for 2 minutes, then whisk in the remaining butter, season and add the tarragon just before serving.

Delicious served with roasted chicken. Also good with fish or pasta. To keep the green colour of the tarragon, don't boil the sauce once it has been added.

Jenny Galloway

Mushroom and St Agur Cheese Sauce

5 **15**

Serves 4

oil for cooking

125g (4oz) button mushrooms

300ml (10fl oz or ½pint) double cream

packet of St Agur cheese

Fry mushrooms in a little olive oil, in a frying pan, until browned.

Add the St Agur cheese, cut into pieces, and the double cream and stir until the cheese has dissolved and the sauce has thickened. Season to taste.

Serve, poured over roasted chicken breasts, wrapped in Parma ham.

Excellent with pasta.

Elizabeth Starbuck, Nottingham

Pesto Chicken and Potato Salad

15 20

Serves 4

500g (1lb 2oz) unpeeled new potatoes

350g (12oz) skinned, cooked chicken, cut into cubes
(about 3 breasts)

125g (4 - 6 oz) baby spinach leaves

1 small lemon - juice only

3 tabs olive oil

2 tabs pesto (from a jar is fine)

Boil the potatoes in a saucepan of salted water for 15 minutes.

Drain and roughly crush with a fork. Not too much.

Tip the cooked chicken into the pan, and scatter in the baby spinach leaves. Gently mix together, using a large spoon.

Make the dressing by mixing the lemon juice, olive oil and pesto together. Pour onto the ingredients in the pan. Stir gently to coat the other ingredients.

Season to taste.

Serve in bowls.

....

Variations: Use rocket or watercress instead of spinach.
Add cold poached salmon instead of chicken.

Vegetarian option: leave out the chicken and add chopped spring
onions, peas, asparagus or toasted pine nuts to the potatoes and leaves.

A taste of Southern Italy

Spicy Sauce for Chicken Barbecue

10 | (25

Serves 4
Needs at least 2 hours to marinate

4 chicken breasts cut into chunks

300ml (10fl oz) orange juice

150ml (5fl oz) soy sauce

2 tabs runny honey

2 cloves of garlic, crushed

freshly milled black pepper

pinch of chilli; or 1 tab sweet chilli sauce

1 tab cooking oil (groundnut or sunflower)

1 tab ready mixed Dijon mustard

2 tabs grated ginger

Pre-heat a moderate oven to 180°C/ 360F/Gas 4

Whisk all the marinade ingredients together in a bowl, and pour over the chicken chunks to marinate for several hours.

Soak 4 skewers in cold water to stop them burning on the barbecue. Thread the chunks of chicken on to the skewers and leave in the fridge until ready to cook.

Heat the remainder of the marinade to boiling point, where it is thickening, and serve as a sauce.

Whole chicken breasts can also be used. Marinate and cook in the oven for 25 minutes.

Serve with a crisp salad and French bread to soak up the juices.
Easy recipe. Good for men to cook on the barbecue!
Vegetarian option: marinated Quorn works well.

Chris Smith, Gedling

Piquant Fruity Sauce

10   **15**

Serves 4

125g (4oz) fresh cranberries

2 cooking apples; Bramleys are best

100g (3oz) caster sugar

Combine the fresh cranberries, peeled and cored chopped apples, with the sugar. Cook over a low heat until the fruit softens but still holds its shape.

Add more sugar if the sauce is too sharp.

Serve with goose or turkey. Also good with pork

Rosemary Jarman

Canard Lorange

20   **20-25**

Serves 4

½ tab brown sugar

55ml (2fl oz) white wine vinegar

250ml (8fl oz) orange juice

250ml (8fl oz) chicken stock

1 orange, zest finely sliced

2 oranges, segmented

Put sugar and vinegar into a pan and bring to the boil.

Reduce, until sauce begins to caramelise but don't let it burn.

Add orange juice and reduce to a third.

Add chicken stock. Leave to simmer for 5 minutes.

Add orange segments and poach for 20-30 seconds.

To serve: place orange segments around the duck and the sauce around the plate.

Also good with goose.
Adapted from a well known recipe but still worth making

Roasted Duck Breasts with Apricot Sauce

Serves 2 - easily doubled

2 duck breasts
(around 200g/7oz)

1 tsp clear honey

250g (9oz) fresh apricots,
stoned and halved

55ml (2fl oz) dry white wine

100ml (3½fl oz) water

1 tab brown sugar

salt and pepper

Pre-heat oven to 180C/360F/Gas4

Pat duck breasts dry with kitchen roll and slash skins with diagonal cuts 1cm apart. Place on a rack over a roasting pan, skin side up, and prick skins to release the fat. Season and smear with honey.

Place in centre of oven for 15 minutes.

Remove from oven. Place rack on a baking tray and pour off fat from the roasting pan. Place apricot halves in the bottom of the pan and add wine and water. Return to the oven, with the rack of duck breasts above, for 15 minutes, if you like your duck pink or 25 minutes if well done.

Remove from oven. Transfer the rack of duck to a baking tray and leave to rest in a warm place while you make the sauce.

Spoon off any excess fat from the pan. Pass apricots and juice through a medium sieve and return to the roasting pan.

Add brown sugar, seasoning and a little water if the sauce is too thick.

Slice duck along diagonals and serve with the sauce separately.

Jan Lindsay

...a collection of Delicious Sauce Recipes

Duck Breasts with Red Currant Jelly Sauce

5   **25**

Serves 4

4 ducks breasts

2 tabs oil

1 red onion, finely chopped

6 tabs red currant jelly

6 tabs red wine vinegar

2 oranges, juice only

seasoning

Pan fry the duck as you like it.

Heat the oil in a pan over a medium heat. Add the onions and cook for 5 minutes until softened but not browned. Add the jelly, vinegar and orange juice.

Bring to the boil and reduce for 5 minutes until the mixture is syrupy. Add seasoning and taste.

Drizzle around the duck slices or breasts.
Equally good with goose or turkey.

A slug of port, added with the jelly, really livens up this sauce!

Carol

Plum Sauce

15 **20-30**

Serves 4 - 6

glug of oil

1 shallot or ½ small onion, finely chopped

1 garlic clove, crushed and finely chopped

500g (1lb 2oz) plums, stoned and chopped

2 tabs Muscavado sugar

1 tab dark Soy sauce

1 tab light Soy sauce

1 level tab Chinese five-spice powder

2 tsps balsamic vinegar

Heat oil in a pan over a medium heat and add the shallot (or onion) and cook gently until softened.

Add the garlic. Stir in the plums and sugar. Cover and simmer until the plums soften and the mixture thickens.

Stir in the soy sauce, five-spice powder and balsamic vinegar.

Simmer for 5 minutes.

Taste and adjust seasoning or add sugar to your taste.

Excellent with duck breasts, turkey, pheasant or any game.
Also good with fillet steaks or pork.
Serve with mixed greens or stir-fried vegetables.

Origin unknown

THE WINE TASTING
It has a nose of rotting cabbage and
hangs in the mouth
like a dead hedgehog . . .
"Never mind the price I will have six Cases"
1998

Succulent, Sizzling Meats

Lamb Casserole with Port

10 **105**

Serves 4

750g (1½ lbs) lean, cubed lamb

½ small onion, finely chopped

1 tab plain flour

500ml (¾ pint) lamb stock or chicken stock

300ml (10fl or ½ pint) Ruby Port (cheapest available)

1 tab red currant jelly

1 tab mint jelly

1 tab olive or sunflower oil

Pre-heat oven to 180C/360F/Gas 4

Heat oil in an ovenproof casserole dish and brown the lamb in batches. Remove from the pan and keep warm. Add the onion and stir well. Return the lamb to the pan; add the flour, coating the meat. Add the stock, port and jellies; stir well. Bring to simmering point and add seasoning, if required.

Cover and place in the oven for 1½ hours or until tender but don't let it dry out.

Check and stir occasionally, adding a little boiling water if necessary.

Taste before serving; you might want to add more red currant or mint jelly.

Serve with creamy mash and seasonal vegetables.

Very rich and delicious!

Carol Mountjoy

Apple and Mustard Cider Gravy

15 **20-25**

Serves 4

25g (1oz) butter

1 large onion, finely chopped

1 tsp sugar

1 medium sized Bramley apple, chopped into small chunks

1 tsp thyme leaves

2 tsps plain flour

250mls (8fl oz) chicken stock

250mls (8fl oz) dry cider

1 to 2 tsps of Dijon mustard

Melt butter in a medium saucepan. Add onion and sugar.

Cover saucepan and cook slowly until golden.

You might need to add a little stock if it becomes too dry.

Add apple chunks and thyme and cook until soft.

Sprinkle flour over mixture and add stock and cider and cook, stirring occasionally.

Allow sauce to cool a little and blitz.

Good with pork and gammon.
Get ahead: make the day before and reheat.

From Normandy, France

Cumberland Sauce

20 **25**

Serves 4

450g (1lb) red currant jelly

rind of 1 orange

rind of 1 lemon

juice of 2 oranges

juice of 2 lemons

2 rounded tsps of cornflour (or arrowroot)

2 large glasses of port

Pare the rinds of the orange and lemon thinly. Cut into fine shreds and blanch for 5 minutes in boiling water.

Strain and refresh in cold water.

Put the jelly in a pan with the strained fruit juice. Bring to the boil; simmer for 3 minutes. Add the port.

Mix the cornflour with a little cold water. Stir into the boiling liquid and remove immediately from the heat. Keep stirring until the sauce has thickened. Strain, cover and cool.

Add the blanched rind.

Get ahead: make the day before it is to be used. Serve warm or cold.

The best ever sauce for ham.

A Parisian maître d'hôtel, on being complimented on this Cumberland sauce recipe remarked,

"The secret, is the addition of two tablespoons of Grand Marnier, it makes all the difference"

...and it does!

Gilly Cross

Paprika Pork Kebabs

15 **20-30**

Serves 4
Marinate for 2 hours

4 pork loin steaks, cubed

4-5 tabs rapeseed oil or olive oil

4 tabs paprika

1 inch fresh ginger, peeled and grated

1 tab wholegrain mustard

2 garlic cloves, crushed

1 tab balsamic vinegar

ground black pepper

If using the oven: pre-heat to 180C/360F/Gas 4

Put the cubed pork into a non-metallic bowl and add all the remaining ingredients. Using a spoon or your hands, thoroughly coat the pork. Cover the bowl and refrigerate for 2 hours or overnight for the flavours to develop.

If using wooden skewers, soak for 15-20 minutes to prevent burning when barbecuing. Skewer the marinated pork with a selection of cubed summer vegetables, such as: mushrooms, courgettes, tomatoes, fennel, peppers etc.

Barbecue - basting occasionally, until thoroughly cooked.

Or cook in the oven for 20-30 minutes.

Serve with a summer salad of mixed leaves
Vegetarian option: *leave out the pork and use as a basting sauce with the vegetables of your choice.*

Hungarian based dish

Beer and Mustard Sauce

Serves 2

1 onion finely chopped

15ml (1 tab) cooking oil

15ml (1 tab) French mustard

150ml (¼ pint) Guinness or brown ale

2 tabs clear honey

juice of ½ lemon

salt and pepper to taste

Gently fry the onion in oil for five minutes.

Add all the remaining ingredients and bring to the boil.

Reduce heat and simmer for five minutes.

Serve hot.

Serve with grilled meats.
Great for barbecues.

From a keen barbecuer.....!

Cherry and Pinot Noir Reduction

Serves 4

2 shallots finely chopped

3 tabs unsalted butter

2 small glasses Pinot Noir or Merlot

1 tin cherries (24 fresh, pitted cherries)

3 tabs chicken stock

Gently sauté the shallots in 2 tabs of butter but don't allow the butter to brown.

Add wine, cherries and chicken stock. Cook the sauce for 10 to15 minutes, until reduced to a thick and creamy consistency (the consistency of heated jam).

Leave to one side while the steaks are cooking.

Before serving, return to a gentle heat and add 1 tab of butter.

Serve over steak
This tasty sauce will wake up any steak or indeed any red meat.
Kate Kemp

Smoked Bacon, Horseradish & Guinness Sauce for Fillet or Rump Steak

10 **35**

Serves 2

4 rashers of smoked bacon, cut in julienne (small strips)

1 small red onion, sliced

1 clove of garlic, chopped

200ml (8fl oz) Guinness

200ml (8fl oz) of beef stock

1 tsp horseradish sauce - or to your taste

2 tsps double cream

1 knob of butter

1 tab chopped parsley

2 steaks

Pan fry or grill steaks to your liking.

Sauté bacon and onion until golden brown. Add garlic and cook for a few minutes, being careful not to burn the garlic, as it will taste bitter.

Deglaze the pan with Guinness and reduce sauce by one third.

Add the beef stock; simmer for 15 minutes.

Add the horseradish to taste. Simmer for another 5 minutes until reduced to a syrupy consistency.

Whisk in the cream and the knob of butter.

Season to taste and finish with the chopped parsley.

A luscious sauce!

Can also be served with game and venison.

The Martins Arms, Colston Bassett

Hot Olive and Caper Sauce

Serves 6

250ml (8fl oz) extra virgin oil

300g (10oz) small Italian black and green olives in brine, rinsed

10 salted anchovy fillets, rinsed and roughly chopped

3 tabs salted capers, rinsed and chopped

2 garlic cloves, peeled and finely chopped

150ml (5¼fl oz) double cream

freshly ground black pepper

Heat the olive oil in a small pan until very hot.

Add the olives, anchovies, capers and garlic.

Cook for 2 minutes, stirring, just to soften the garlic.

Remove from the heat and allow to cool briefly.

Add the cream, stirring gently as the sauce thickens.

Season with black pepper.

A very unusual complement with steak
From an unknown Italian restaurant

Katia's Mushroom Sauce

Serves 2 – 3

50g (2 oz) mushrooms

1 onion

125ml (4fl oz) double cream

150ml (5fl oz) soured cream

1 tab butter

Chop the mushrooms and onion.

Melt the butter in a pan, and soften the onions, adding the mushrooms after a few minutes.

Gradually add the double cream and soured cream.

Bring to the boil and reduce until a coating consistency.

Add seasoning and serve.

Quick and easy. Good with steak or chicken. Try it with pasta.

Sal Marks from the charity 'Guys'

Beef Steak Topping

grill the steaks to your liking

Serves 4

1½ tabs English mustard powder

1 tab horseradish sauce (strong)

2 tabs Worcestershire sauce

40g (1½oz) butter, softened a little

4 beef steaks of your choice

Mix the mustard powder, horseradish sauce, Worcester sauce and butter in a bowl, until soft. Heat the grill or frying pan, spread the mixture onto the chosen steaks and cook in the usual way.

Being careful, if the grill is too hot, the topping will burn!

Delicious! This makes a very good, quick supper dish, with oven chips, mushrooms and a green vegetable.
Vegetarian option: preheat oven to (180C/360F/Gas 4)
Spread the mixture inside the tops of Portobello mushrooms and cook for 20 minutes or so.

Sheila Johnson

Quick and Simple Steak Marinade

Serves 1 - easily doubled

1 tsp olive oil

½ tsp soy sauce

2 dashes Worcester sauce

freshly ground black pepper

Mix the olive oil, soy sauce and Worcester sauce together.

Brush the mixture over both sides of the steak.

Leave to marinate for at least 10 minutes.

Grind black pepper over the steaks before frying or BBQ

Quick and easy way of adding flavour.

The Lazy Cook!

...a collection of Delicious Sauce Recipes

' The perfect
    hostess "

Asian Delights

Asian Dressing for Green Salad

15

Makes enough for the green salad but - easily doubled

Dressing

2 tabs lime juice

1 tab fish sauce (optional)

1 tab dark brown soft sugar

1½ tabs rice vinegar (or white wine vinegar)

ground black pepper

a little chilli, fresh or dry to add heat (optional)

Mix all ingredients and make sure that the sugar has dissolved.

Store in the fridge; keeps well for 3-4 days

Suggested green salad

sugar snap peas

small red onion

baby leaf or tender leaf mixed salad

chopped coriander or parsley

ground black pepper,

sea salt

Blanch sugar snap peas for 1 minute; drain; rinse until cold, then slice, diagonally, in two.

Chop onion into thin rings.

Mix together salad leaves, onion, coriander (or parsley).

Add Asian dressing just before serving and toss well. May be served as a salad on its own or as a side dish with fish, chicken or meat.

Adapted recipe from a Singapore restaurant

Sauce for King Prawns

20   **60**

Serves 4-6

150ml (5fl oz) oil

174g (6oz) shallots, chopped

I small chilli, finely chopped

2 inches fresh ginger, peeled and grated

2 garlic cloves, finely chopped

1 stick lemongrass, crushed

2 lime leaves, optional

20ml (1 tab) fish sauce, optional

2 tsps crushed and roasted coriander seeds

2 tsps tumeric

275ml (½ pint) fish or veg stock (plus extra water)

ground black pepper and a good pinch of salt

Heat the oil in a pan, add the shallots and cook until softened.

Add the lime leaves.   Add the chilli, ginger, lemongrass and garlic to the pan with the shallots. Put in the rest of the ingredients and simmer gently for 50 minutes to an hour, until well reduced. Stir, occasionally, adding extra water if necessary.

Add the salt at the end of cooking time. Remove the lime leaves.

Serve the sauce with shelled and de-veined king prawns.

....

This has a good Thai flavour. Serve with basmati rice.

From the Head Chef in Kaspar's Seafood Bar, the Savoy Hotel, London

Prawn Curry Sauce

10 **25**

Serves 2 - easily doubled

50g (2oz) butter

1 small chopped onion

1 tab curry powder (to your taste)

1 level tab of plain flour

150ml (5fl oz) light stock

juice of half a lemon

4 ripe tomatoes (skinned and chopped)

pinch salt

150g (5oz) cooked prawns

splash single cream

Sauté onion in butter until soft.

Add curry powder, then the flour. Cook for 1 minute.

Add the stock, lemon juice, salt and tomatoes.

Put the lid on the saucepan and simmer on a very low heat for about 20 minutes, stirring occasionally.

Add the prawns and cream.

Cook for 2 to 3 minutes until prawns are hot.

Serve with plain rice garnished with lemon strips.

Also good with chicken.

Easy and tasty.

Vegetarian option: leave out the prawns and serve as a sauce for vegetable curry.

Elizabeth Alcock

Dry Mix For Tandoori Sauce

This dry mix keeps well and matures well

20g (¾oz) mango powder

30g (1oz) paprika (the new smoked one works scrumily!)

30g (1oz) ground coriander

20g (¾oz) dried mint

20g (¾oz) beetroot powder (optional)

15g (½oz) chilli powder

30g (1oz) ground cumin

10g (¼oz) annatto seed (from Asian/Indian shops)

salt to taste.

Mix all ingredients and store in an air tight container.

Use as required.

Should last 10 to 12 months.

Sea salt is good with added turmeric, fenugreek, ground almond and dried mint.   Pinch of each to 5g of sea salt... and voila! Aromatic salt.

If you want it red? A la restaurant? Add food colourant.

Happy saucyness!

Steve and Sue Piper

...a collection of Delicious Sauce Recipes

Grilled Asian Pork with Peanut Butter

15 **20**

Serves 4
Marinate for at least 2 hours

2 small pork tenderloins

Sauce

1 can 400g light coconut milk

125g (4oz) smooth peanut butter

125ml (4fl oz) soy sauce

3 tabs lime juice

3 tabs brown sugar

2 large garlic cloves, crushed and finely chopped

2 tsps chopped coriander

Butterfly the pork tenderloins, open out, and bat in between 2 pieces of cling film until ½ inch thick. Put in a non-metallic dish.

Whisk the sauce ingredients until smooth, pour over the pork and marinate for several hours.

Drain off the excess sauce, heat the grill and when hot, put the pork under for 5 - 7 minutes, turning once during cooking.

Put the remaining sauce into a saucepan. Add 2 tabs water and bring to the boil, until thick. Add more water if necessary to give the consistency of thick cream. Serve with the sauce poured over the pork or served separately.

....

Pork may be cooked on a barbecue.

Averil Johnson

Khmer Sauce for Fish or Chicken Amok

Serves 4
Marinate for 10 minutes

2 tabs lemon grass paste

2 peeled cloves garlic

2 shallots, peeled and finely chopped

1 tab finely chopped galangal

1 tab finely chopped fresh ginger

2 red chillies, deseeded – or to your taste

½ tab turmeric

2 kaffir lime leaves, shredded

2 tabs vegetable oil

200ml (7fl oz) coconut cream

1-2 tabs palm sugar (or light Muscavado sugar)

¼ tsp shrimp paste (optional)

1 tab fish sauce (optional)

1 beaten egg

salt to taste

Blend lemongrass paste, garlic, shallots, galangal, ginger, chillies, turmeric, and kaffir lime leaves with 1-2 tabs of oil until smooth.

Add coconut cream, salt, sugar, shrimp paste, fish sauce, beaten egg and mix well.   Transfer to a pan.

Marinate pieces of fish or chicken in the sauce for 10 minutes.

Cook on the hob, gentle to moderate heat - about 15 minutes for the fish and 20 minutes for the chicken or until cooked.

Serve with rice or noodles and finely shredded firm mango.
Easy, fragrant and utterly delicious!

Janet Madden

Indian Green Masala Sauce

25

Serves 2 very generously

1 tab coriander seeds

1 tab ground turmeric

½ tab cumin seeds

¼ tab cloves (optional)

1 cinnamon stick

handful of fresh green chillies, coarsely chopped

a few cloves of garlic peeled

a finger sized piece of peeled root ginger

200g (7oz) chopped red onion

1 mint sprig

bunch of fresh coriander leaves (or parsley)

a little sugar

water

tin of coconut milk

splash of oil for cooking

Put all dried spices in a frying pan (no oil) and cook over a low heat until they crackle, stirring as they cook.

Put all ingredients in a food processor with a little water and blitz to smooth paste.

Heat a little oil in a suitable pan, add the paste and cook for a few minutes.

Add diluted coconut milk – that's 2 parts water to 1 part coconut milk (which prevents the sauce from curdling)

Add your choice of meat, fish or vegetables and simmer gently until cooked. No need to seal the meat before placing in the sauce.

Especially good with humongously large prawns!
Also, a really good vegetarian option.

Steve and Sue Piper

Thai Ginger and Honey Dressing

Serves 4 - easily doubled

1 tsp chopped fresh ginger

2 tsps (20ml) clear, runny honey

2 tsps walnut, grapeseed or light olive oil

½ lime, juice only

Combine all the ingredients until thoroughly mixed.

Tangy and fresh.

May be served chilled or slightly warm.
Drizzle over fish, fishcakes; serve as a dipping sauce for large prawns or sweet potato wedges...... anything that needs a ginger hit!

London Thai Restaurant

Mango and Chilli Sauce

Very easy
Serves 4

1 mango, peeled and diced

1 red onion, peeled and sliced

freshly chopped coriander - to your taste

sweet chilli sauce - to your taste

a little lime zest and juice - to your taste

Mix all the ingredients together. Transfer to a serving dish and sprinkle lime zest over the top.

Use as a side dish for Asian recipes.

Perks up hot or cold salmon.

Perfect with pork. Delicious with hot or cold chicken, roasted aubergines......
eat on its own ....or with a green salad.

Rosemary Jarman

Satay Sauce

Serves 4

200ml (7fl oz) coconut cream

4 tabs crunchy peanut butter

1 tsp Worcestershire sauce

few drops of Tabasco sauce

fresh coconut to garnish
(optional)

Pour the coconut cream into a small saucepan and heat gently for about 2 minutes.

Add the Worcestershire sauce and Tabasco sauce to taste.

Add the peanut butter and stir vigorously until the mixture is thoroughly blended. Continue to heat but do not allow to boil.

Use a potato peeler to shave thin strips from a piece of fresh coconut, if using. Pour into serving bowls.

Scatter the coconut over the sauce and serve immediately.

This is a speedy and delicious sauce to serve with barbecued skewers of chicken or pork. Also good with barbecued vegetables.
Thai restaurant in K.L.

Cucumber and Ginger Raita

30 for cucumber to degorge

Serves 6-8

1 cucumber

1 tab grated ginger

1 tsp toasted and crushed cumin seeds

400 ml (14fl oz) Greek Yoghurt

chopped mint (optional)

Grate the cucumber and sprinkle with salt, leave on a flat plate, tilted slightly, for 30 minutes to draw the juices out.

Wash and dry the cucumber, mix with the rest of the ingredients.

Season and serve in small bowls as a dip or an accompaniment.

Can add chopped mint as an option.

Delicious accompaniment with lamb and any type of curry.

A well known and popular recipe

Steve's Masala Mix

Serves 2 to 3

2 whole dried red chillies; according to taste

7 tabs oil - olive or vegetable

¾ tsp Garam Masala

1 level tsp tumeric

¼ tsp carom seeds crushed (optional)

1 tabs dried fenugreek

1 level tsp cumin seeds

½ tsp coriander seeds

1 medium sized onion, chop half in chunks; other half really small

1 tsp garlic and ginger paste (make more; it freezes well)

½ tsp fresh green chilli paste

¾ tsp of red chilli powder. Don't skimp. Buy good stuff!

25g (1oz) butter diced into little chunks

salt to taste....

200g (7oz) peeled plum tomatoes

60g (2oz) each green, red and yellow peppers, cut into strips

raw king prawns (or ready cooked prawns) or poached chicken

2 tabs fresh coriander (or parsley)

Have all ingredients measured or weighed and prepared to hand.

Heat oil over medium heat for about half a minute.

Add whole dried red chillies, fenugreek, coriander, carom and cumin seeds. Cook until sizzling. Add onion. Cook, stirring continuously until onion is nearly brown and caramilising.

Add garlic, ginger paste and tomatoes; then red chilli powder, salt, butter and turmeric. Cook for 5 - 6 minutes.

Add water if the mix gets a bit sticky. Sauce is now cooked.

(Oil might separate a little at this stage).

Add peppers and cook for 10 minutes.

If using as a vegetarian option: serve now with plain rice.

If using prawns, add now and cook. Prawns will turn pink.

If using chicken: cook by poaching first before adding to the sauce. Steam for a further 2 minutes. Tin foil on top works well. Add coriander and cook for a further minute.

*Serve with plain rice
....and enjoy!!*

Sue Piper

Delicious, Dazzling Desserts... Sauces, Custards, Creams, Possets and Puddings

Affogato

5

Serves 2 - very easy

2 scoops vanilla ice cream
(home made or top quality)

2 tabs Kahlua or Tia Maria
liqueur

75mls (2½fl oz) strong
espresso coffee

Put 2 scoops of ice cream in 2 coffee
cups or glasses.

Warm the Khalua (or Tia Maria) with
the coffee until hot but not boiling.

Pour over the ice cream.

Serve with biscotti.

No time to make a dessert? Try Affogato at the end of your meal instead.

First tried at the Martins Arms

Butterscotch Sauce

2 **10**

Makes 300ml (about ½ pint) easily doubled

75g (3oz) light Muscovado sugar

150ml (5fl oz) double cream

50g (2oz) butter (1oz is fine)

I tab water

Put the sugar in a saucepan over a
medium heat and add the water.
Stir all the time until the sugar has
dissolved.

Bring to the boil and cook for
5-7 minutes until you have a darkish
caramel. Watch the sauce carefully
and **don't let it burn.**

Remove from the heat and whisk in the
cream, then the butter until the sauce
is smooth and glistening.

At this stage the sauce may be cooled
and gently reheated before serving.

*Drizzle over ice cream, bread and butter pudding, sticky toffee pudding, apple pies,
fruit... or anything that takes your fancy! It is wonderful!*

Bunty

Toffee Apple Sauce

Serves 4 - easily doubled

2 medium Granny Smith apples

75g (3oz) butter

150g (5oz) light Muscovado sugar

150ml (5fl oz or ¼ pint) double cream

Serve the hot toffee sauce over winter puddings, ice cream, fruit pies and tarts – even fresh fruit. This wonderful sauce is utterly delicious! Easily reheated.

Unknown but passed on from a friend

Peel, core and cut the apples into 5mm dice. Place the apples in a heavy based pan with the butter and sugar and heat gently until the butter has melted and sugar dissolved.

Increase the heat and cook on high for about 5 minutes until the colour of the sauce begins to darken.

Do not let it burn.

Remove from the heat. Add the cream. Return to the heat, stirring gently, all the time until the sauce bubbles.

Chocolate Sauce

Serves 4

125g (4oz) plain chocolate

30g (1oz) caster sugar

150ml (5fl oz or ¼ pint milk)

2 level tsps cornflour

4 tabs water

150ml (¼ pint) double cream

rum or brandy to taste (optional)

Place chocolate and water in a pan and melt.

Mix cornflour with the milk. Add sugar, cornflour and milk to the chocolate mixture and stir until gently boiling.

Boil for 1 minute to cook the cornflour.

If it is to be served hot, add the cream without boiling.

If serving cold: allow the sauce to cool, then, add the cream and the rum or brandy to taste.

Delicious served with vanilla ice cream or as a dipping sauce for whole fresh strawberries.... or anything else that takes your fancy!

Margaret Pollett

Hot Fudge Sauce

25

Serves 6 good servings

225g (8oz) butter

125g (4oz) unsweetened cocoa powder

125g (4oz) white sugar

1 can (300ml or ½ pint) evaporated milk

1 tsp of instant coffee powder

175g (6oz) chocolate chips

1 tsp vanilla extract

dash of salt

Sift the cocoa with the sugar.

Combine butter, cocoa, sugar evaporated milk and instant coffee in a saucepan over medium heat. Bring to the boil and boil for 10 minutes; whisk while cooking.

Remove from the heat; stir in the chocolate chips, vanilla and salt.

The sauce will thicken as it cools.

Serve immediately or store in the fridge until ready to use.

Wonderful served warm over ice cream. Also good cold as a cake filling. Good with anything that needs a very chocolatey sauce!
Maria Jackson, Langar and U.S.A.

Passion Fruit Butter

10 **4**

Makes about 2 jars

3 eggs

125g (4oz) white caster sugar

200ml (6-7fl oz) passion fruit pulp (about 6 passion fruit)

125g (4oz) unsalted butter, melted

Beat the eggs and then beat in the sugar.

Add the passion fruit juice and butter.

Microwave everything for about four minutes or until it has thickened.

Delicious spread on toasted bread. Also good used as cake fillings.
Keeps in the fridge for up for 2 weeks.

Janet

Homemade Peanut Butter

300g serving - very easy

300g (10 oz) roasted peanuts (salted or unsalted; to your taste)

60ml (2fl oz) vegetable oil

1 tab honey (optional and to your taste; add more or less)

Place peanuts into a food processor and blitz for a minute or so.

The peanuts should be forming a ball.

Continue processing and check frequently to see if the peanut ball has oil on the top, if not, keep processing.

When the oil appears on top of the ball, pour in the vegetable oil and process for 30 seconds or until creamy.

Add the honey and process for a further 30 seconds.

Store in a sealed container or sterilised jar in the fridge.
Delicious spread on bread, toast, in satay sauces – the list is endless!

Jan Burdett
'Jan's Homemade Bakes', Hose, Nottinghamshire

Cinnamon Butter

Makes about 6 tablespoons

4 tabs softened butter

2 tsps ground cinnamon

2 tabs icing sugar (or to your taste)

Blend all ingredients and chill until required.

Delicious on toasted bread, muffins or crumpets. Try it on pancakes.
Keeps in the fridge for about 1 week.

A Cotswold Bakery

Mango Fool

Serves 4 to 6 depending on the portion size

4 ripe mangos

150ml (5fl oz or ¼ pint) whipping or double cream.

1 unwaxed lemon, zest and juice (or lime)

caster sugar to taste

Peel the mango. Slice into pieces and whizz to a puree in a food processor. Sieve the puree (or not, as you prefer)

Whip the cream to soft peaks. Add the mango puree, finely zested lemon rind and lemon juice to the cream and fold in gently. Sweeten according to taste.

Pour into glasses or small, pretty serving bowls and chill.

Serve with tiny sweet, dessert biscuits. Fools are traditionally served in summer but are also good after a spicy, main course.

Bunty

Lemon Syllabub

Serves 6 to 8

300ml (10fl oz) whipping cream

300ml (10fl oz) double cream

2 unwaxed lemons, zest and juice

50g (2oz) caster sugar

55ml (2fl oz) sherry, of your choice

Combine the creams and lightly whisk together.

Add the finely zested lemon rind, lemon juice, sherry and sugar to the cream. Beat until the soft peak stage

Don't beat too much; the syllabub will thicken as it chills.

Half fill small, pretty, glasses or ramekins.

Cover with cling film and chill until ready to serve.

Garnish with edible flowers. De-lusciuos!
From an old Elizabethan recipe. "Bub" is an Elizabethan word for drink.

Apricot Cream

10-15

Serves 6 in small glasses, cups or bowls

120ml (4fl oz) double cream

2 tabs Bonne Maman apricot preserve

squeeze lime juice

glug of Gran Marnier, apple brandy or your choice

Quick, easy, smooth and delicious. Serve with tiny, sweet biscuits. Wonderful with sieved passion fruit juice drizzled over the top just before serving.

Bunty

Put the apricot preserve into a small bowl and microwave until the preserve has just 'loosened' a little.

Do not overheat.

Sieve the preserve into a clean bowl if you want the end results to be smooth. If you don't mind the apricot pieces, then, don't bother.

Whip the double cream until it just holds its shape - but no more.

Add the preserve, lime juice and Gran Marnier (or liquor of your choice) and gently fold into the cream until well mixed and smooth.

Spoon into small, individual glasses, pretty cups or bowls and garnish with raspberries and a dusting of icing sugar.

Banana Cream

5-10

Serves 6 to 8 depending on portion size

2 large or 3 small bananas

150ml (¼ pint) natural yoghurt

150ml (¼ pint) double cream

sunflower seeds – optional

Peel the bananas. Put into a blender or liquidiser with the yoghurt and blitz well. Whip the cream until stiff and fold into the banana mixture.

Top with sunflower seeds or nuts of your choice.

Add to any fruit dessert or ......simply serve on its own!

`Luscious!`

Quick and easy. A childhood treat – well known but quick and simple.

Coffee Cream

5

Servings vary according to use

1 tub Mascarpone cheese

2 tsps icing sugar (to your taste)

2 tsps Camp coffee essence (more if you wish)

walnuts (optional)

Gently, beat mascarpone cheese and coffee essence together.

Sift icing sugar into the cream and mix together.

Fold in walnuts (if using).

Keeps well in the fridge for 3-4 days, covered with cling film.

Wonderful as a soft, luscious, topping for carrot cake; toppings and fillings for sponge cakes; coffee and walnut cake; filling meringues, cupcakes...

Celia Wallwin, Newlands

Elderflower Posset

15-20

Serves 4 - 6 portions

300ml (10fl oz) double cream

75g (3oz) caster sugar

juice and zest of half an unwaxed lemon

75ml (2-3fl oz) elderflower cordial; according to taste

Pour the cream into a saucepan; add the sugar and zest.

Slowly bring to the boil, stirring to dissolve the sugar.

Boil for 2-3 minutes, stirring all the time. Remove from the heat.

Stir in the lemon juice and cordial. The sauce should thicken.

Strain into a jug to remove the zest.

Pour into small glasses or ramekins and allow to cool.

When completely cool, cover with cling film and chill.

Dust with icing sugar and serve with berries of your choice, almond or dessert biscuits. Creamy and luscious.
Get ahead *and make the day before.*

Colston Bassett Springtime Recipe

Luscious Lemon Posset with Raspberry Coulis

10 **10**

Serves 4 or 8 eggcups (easily doubled)

300ml (½ pint) double cream

75g (3oz) sugar

1 to 2 lemons - zest and juice

Pour cream into a saucepan and add sugar and zest.

Slowly bring to the boil, stirring constantly to dissolve the sugar. Once boiling let the cream bubble for a further 3-4 minutes, stirring all the time. Remove from heat.

Add juice of 1 lemon stirring constantly.

The sauce should thicken. Taste; add more juice if necessary.

It should taste sweet, tangy and creamy. Strain into a jug to remove zest. Cool for 4 to 5 minutes and pour into small glasses (or egg cups). Once cool, cover with cling film and chill overnight. Remove from fridge 15 minutes before serving.

A lovely, creamy sauce, which thickens to make an easy, delicious dessert. **Serve** *with almond or dessert biscuits. Wonderful with a layer of raspberry coulis poured over the top.*

Raspberry Coulis

Makes 120ml approx.

300g (10oz) raspberries

125g (4oz) caster sugar; to your taste

squeeze of fresh orange or lemon juice

Cook all ingredients in a pan, over a moderate heat for 5 minutes until raspberries soften. Pass through a fine sieve and leave to cool.

Make in advance.

Keeps in the fridge for 2 days.

From a renowned restaurant along the Thames Valley

...a collection of Delicious Sauce Recipes

Passion Fruit Posset

15-20

Serves 4 - Quick, easy and delicious. Easily doubled

300ml (10fl oz) double cream

70g (about 3oz) caster sugar

3 to 4 passion fruit

I lime - juice only

Scoop out the flesh and juice from 3 passion fruit (use four if you want extra taste) and pass through a sieve, extracting as much juice as possible. Discard the seeds.

Mix with the lime juice.

Pour the cream into a saucepan and add the sugar.

Heat gently, stirring all the time, until the sugar has dissolved.

Bring to the boil and simmer for 3 to 4 minutes, stirring occasionally.

Remove the cream from the heat and stir in the mixed fruit juices.

Allow to cool a little. Pour into ramekins, small teacups or glasses.

When completely cool, cover with cling film.

Chill for at least 6 hours or overnight.

Before serving, split open the remaining passion fruit and spoon over the top of each posset. Serve with tiny biscuits.
Get ahead: make the day before.

A Colston Bassett summer recipe

Stir Fried Bananas and Cashews with Thick Coconut Cream

Serves 4

150g (5oz) unsalted butter

125g (4oz) brown or palm sugar

4 bananas, peeled and cut into 5cm lengths

150g (5oz) of unsalted, roasted cashews

1 lemon, juice and zest

pinch of ground cinnamon or cloves

1 small carton of thick coconut cream

Melt the butter over a gentle heat in a heavy frying pan.

Add the sugar and stir well until combined.

Add the bananas and cashews and gently stir fry until hot and bubbling. Add the lemon zest, juice and cinnamon.

Mix well but gently, so that you do not mash the bananas.

Serve with thick coconut cream.

Just the sort of pudding for after a spicy meal – sublime!

From Australia

Amarula Custard

25

Serves 4

1 vanilla pod

300ml (10fl oz) single cream (or whole milk if preferred)

1 level tab caster sugar

I level tsp cornflour

4 egg yolks

4 tabs Amarula

Split vanilla pod and place in saucepan with the milk.

Slowly bring to the boil. Remove saucepan from heat and leave pod to infuse for 10 minutes. Beat sugar, cornflour and eggs together. Slowly pour in cream or milk, stirring constantly. Transfer to a Bain Marie (or bowl over a pan of gently simmering water).

Stir continuously for 10 minutes or until mixture coats the back of a wooden spoon.

Remove from heat and add the Amarula. Strain and serve.

Delicious poured over fruit, fruit tarts or ice cream.
Quick version: buy good quality vanilla custard.
Heat; add Amarula and serve as above.

Carol Mountjoy
(Recipe originally from Eastern Cape, South Africa)

Jaffa Puddle Pudding

20 · 60

Serves 6 to 8

3 Navel oranges (or large, juicy oranges) zest and juice

1 lemon, juice only

175g (6oz) caster sugar

3 large eggs, separated

50g (2 oz) butter melted; plus extra for greasing

75g (3oz) self raising flour

1 tsp baking powder

250ml (⅓ pint) whole milk or milk with a little added cream

icing sugar for dusting

Pre-heat oven to 180C/360F/Gas 4

Butter an 18cm-20cm deep, oven proof, round soufflé dish

In a bowl, mix the butter, zest and sugar. Beat in the egg yolks.

Mix the citrus juices and milk. Fold in the flour and baking powder. Beat the egg whites to soft peaks and fold gently into the mixture, but make sure that everything is fairly well mixed.

Pour into the buttered soufflé dish. Place in a large roasting tin of hot water. The water should come halfway up the sides of the dish.

Bake for 50 to 55 minutes, or until the top is firm and golden.

Cool slightly, then dust with icing sugar.

A luscious self-saucing pudding. Serve warm; on its own; with cream or ice cream.

Truly wonderful!

Unknown but first tried in Australia

Black Magic Chocolate Pudding

30   (35-40)

Serves 6 to 8 (a puddle of chocolate sauce will form in the pudding base)

200g (7oz) self raising flour

1 tsp baking powder

60g (2oz) cocoa powder

125g (4oz) light Muscovado sugar

170ml (6fl oz) milk

60g (2oz) butter, melted

1 egg, lightly beaten

1 tsp vanilla extract

icing sugar for dusting

For the topping

90g (3oz) light Muscovado sugar

60g (2oz) cocoa powder

Pre-heat the oven to 180C/350F/Gas 4

Butter a 2 litre (18-20cm) deep, round, soufflé dish. Boil a kettle.

Sift the flour, baking powder and cocoa into a bowl. Add the sugar and a pinch of salt. Combine the milk, melted butter, egg and vanilla.

Pour onto the dry ingredients and mix. Pour the mixture into the soufflé dish.

At this stage you can continue or cover with cling film and put into the fridge for 4-5 hours - or overnight.

To continue: mix the topping ingredients and sprinkle over the pudding.

Pour 500ml (18fl oz) of boiling water gently over the top; that's correct!

Put the pudding in a large roasting tin and fill with hot water from the kettle, until it comes half way up the sides of the soufflé dish.

Place on middle shelf of the oven for 35 to 40 minutes until puffy and firm in the centre. Cool slightly and dust with icing sugar.

Note: for a thicker sauce, add slightly less water, or break up a 100g bar of chocolate and add to the mixture before pouring into the soufflé dish.

Serve warm with cream or ice cream. Utterly gorgeous winter pudding!

There are a number of recipes for puddle puddings. This one works well.

Caribbean Pineapple

15-20   15-20

Serves 4-6

1 large, ripe pineapple, peeled; 'eyes' removed

115ml (4fl oz) rum

125g (4oz) butter

80g (2-3oz) light Muscovado sugar; or to your taste

½ lemon, juice only

2 vanilla pods, split and halved

Pre-heat the grill

Slice the pineapple downwards into 8 to 12 long pieces and cut away the core from each slice. Melt the butter in a large frying or ovenproof pan. Lay the pineapple slices in the butter.

Mix the rum and lemon juice and pour over the top. Spread the vanilla between the slices and sprinkle over half the sugar.

Cook over a medium heat, basting from time to time, until the pineapple begins to soften and the sauce is bubbling.

Sprinkle with the remaining sugar and place under a preheated grill until the pineapple becomes nicely caramelised.

Serve on its own with the sauce poured over the top or with a good quality ice cream. Tastes and smells utterly divine!
For a real wow factor, flame in extra rum when you take it to the table.

Carol and Bunty

...a collection of Delicious Sauce Recipes

What's more:

Chrissie Wilson, recently retired Matron from Nottingham City Breast Cancer Ward, is the vital link necessary, in finding the **Home Alone** patients.
Those in need will be given a cheque for £100 to assist in the extra expense when they go home alone from hospital.

Honarary Treasurer: Sheila Johnson
Normanhurst, 175 Derby Road, Chellaston, Derby DE73 57B

Where you can buy this book:

The Golden Cage
99 Derby Road, Nottingham
Tel: 0115 941 1600

Catherine's
718 Mansfield Road, Woodthorpe, Nottingham
Tel: 0115 960 7940

3-7 Church Street, Southwell
Tel: 01636 815 001

195-197 Bramcote Lane, Wollaton
Tel: 0115 928 5110

Find us on Facebook